THE PSYCHODYNAMIC EFFECTS ON THE INTERPRETING PROCESS

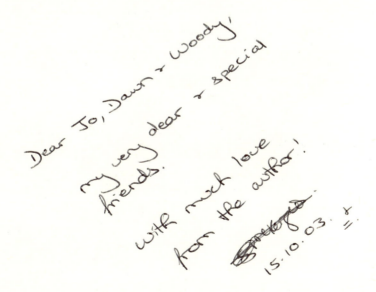

Dear Jo, Dawn & Woody,
my very dear & special
friends.
with much love
from the author!
15.10.03.

THE PSYCHODYNAMIC EFFECTS ON THE INTERPRETING PROCESS

by

Donna L. McKenzie

𝒦𝒫

KISOL PUBLISHERS

British Library Catalouging in Publication Data.
A catalogue record for this book is available from the British Library.

The moral right of the author has been asserted.

ISBN 1-904382-12-6

First Published in 2003 by Kisol Publishers Limited
Cambridge Chambers
200-202 High Street
Bromley
Kent BR1 1PW
United Kingdom.

To Mum

CONTENTS

ACKNOWLEDGEMENTS

I would like to thank the following people for their contribution during my research stages: Carol Padden Associate Professor and Director University of California, San Diego, Marianne Collins-Ahlgren University of Wellington, New Zealand, Doctors Rachel and David Mckee Victoria University of Wellington, Lars Wallin and Ms Anna-Lena Nilsson Stockholm University Institute of Linguists, Mark Marschark Rochester Institute of Technology, Dr Robert Vanderplank University of Oxford Language Centre.

I thank the late Ben Steiner, my mentor at university who encouraged me to have this published. Gratitude to Lisa Mckenzie, my sister, for her amazing skill in taking my concepts and how I required them to be shown on paper and realising this in the form of schematics. Lionel Perks for taking these and creating them in graphic design. Chris Carter must be acknowledged for his immense technical support.

Thanks also to all the individuals who kindly agreed to aid my research by taking part in the introspective research studies, and to Transworld Linguistic Services, London for their assistance. I am indebted to my parents - Billy and Eileen Mckenzie for teaching me the importance of determination and striving to achieve ones best. Also, Anthony Hawkins - my husband, for his patience with the hours that I have spent at my desk and of course his support.

Special thanks however and dedication of this book is to Eileen Mckenzie - my mother. A promise made a long time ago and total appreciation of her unfailing support and belief in me.

PREFACE

The research in this book was initially carried out for the purpose of a thesis for my undergraduate studies. It looked at issues that I found had not been researched before concerning psychodynamic effects on the interpreting situation and I consider it may make a small contribution to the studies of professional development in the field of sign language interpreting.

I was initially steered toward this research topic when I realised that an immense amount of knowledge and information within an interpreting situation is paralinguistic and gained below the language level. It seemed to me that the lexical level is almost secondary, as the lasting impression/intent of the discourse is taken via the meaning, tone and idiosyncrasies of the speaker. If the interpreter's role is to be a conduit for this communication, then these elements must be paramount within the translation.

This led me to consider how the interpreter deduces this paralinguistic information and what devices we all possess in order to relate to this information. Furthermore, it seemed to me that if we can relate to it, then we could have a potential to influence it. Thus the research began.

The main aim was to look at the possible effects that

the presence of an interpreter in any given situation has, specifically concentrating on interpreters of British Sign Language and English. The dynamic effect that the interpreter brings to the situation is the main focus, although what other parties contribute is touched upon throughout. While the interpreting situation can be thought of, in this instance, as a hearing participant, a deaf participant and an interpreter, the effects that are discussed would also be relevant to a group situation.

When the 'deaf participant' is referred to, it should be noted that it is assumed that the individual is using their first or preferred language of British Sign Language (BSL), and identifies him/herself with the Deaf Community, both culturally and linguistically.[1]

---

[1] It is noted that many deaf individuals have acquired BSL as their first language, and that there are many different varieties and modalities of BSL, depending also on how this was acquired. However, outlining these is not the purpose of this research. The reader should note that the interpreter must evaluate and know the language requirements of each individual when interpreting for them, and be aware of the diversity of language needs within this Community. For more information relating to the varieties of BSL please refer to Deuchar 1984, "British Sign Language", p130 - 151. The usual convention of using a capital D for Deaf, to denote membership of a cultural/linguistic group, has not been employed in this book, except where the Deaf Community as a whole is being referred to.

British Sign Language (BSL) is defined as: *"...a visual-gestural language used by many deaf people in Britain as their native language...it is produced in a medium perceived visually, using gestures of the hands and the rest of the body including the face"*. (Deuchar, 1984, p1).

The client group of the BSL/English interpreter that is focused on is the deaf participant, although it must be noted that hearing participants also use the BSL/English interpreter. The reasons for this focus will become apparent, especially within the introspective research chapter.

The interpreter's role is extremely complex for the following reasons. When two strangers meet they make an informed decision as to how each will portray themselves to the other. This is usually based on the type of relationship that they share, the personality that they each have and the social environment that they are in.

When an interpreter is introduced into this equation he/she must take over this portrayal of the persons involved within the communication act, in the way he/she speaks and acts. Jung describes this as the portrayal of the "persona".

"Our persona is the appearance we present to the world. It is the character we assume, through it, we relate to others". (Fadiman and Frager 1994, p.71)

The interpreting role therefore enters the realm of psychodynamics which is explained by Cheshire (1975, p.2) as those dynamics *"which deal with the interplay of such mental states and forces as regularly influence, and sometimes dominate, our actions and experience"*.

The focus in this study, therefore, was to understand the psychodynamics rather than to evaluate how exactly the interpreter translates source language (sL) into target language (tL). Many models have been created in order to illustrate the process of interpreting but here it is important for us to look at what possible effects are produced within the interpreting process by the very fact that every person is an individual. For this reason, a very simplistic model was chosen; that of the monolingual communication act (Fig 3.1.1). This model expands into the translation-communicative process (Fig 3.1.2) which does not give information as to how the interpreter encodes the information, but does show the complexity of the translation process as illustrated in Fig 4.1. These models will be introduced within chapter one.

In order to underpin the research study and to gain insight into the field of psychodynamics, a review was done of work already carried out by established psychologists relating to personality, perception and schematic and cognitive influences. The first part of this study, therefore, focuses on and clarifies the relevant concepts and theories, so that my research findings, and the possible effects that the interpreter has can then be looked at and understood in the light of these.

My initial hypothesis and objectives for this research were as follows:

"The diversity of human beings and their cognitive experiences result in a community of individuals.

These individuals present themselves to the world as they wish to do so. With the introduction of an interpreter taking over this portrayal an impact or dynamic effect is made upon the situation. If that interpreter was not present, these effects would not be evident in the same way".

Objectives: To seek answers to the following questions

1. Do the culturally specific cognitive experiences of the Deaf community contribute to particular dynamic effects?
2. Do the attitudes of some interpreters contribute to these effects and are there implications relating to their training?
3. Do the elements of language perception of the interpreter and of the deaf client influence com munication breakdown?

The methodology used was that of quantitative and qualitative research. Introspective research methods were used in order for results to be more detailed and personal from each participant. The field of spoken language interpreting was also researched, in order to analyse whether the effects were similar or different within the visual and spoken field of interpreting

Visual representation through graphs and diagrams has been incorporated throughout in order to clarify concepts portrayed. This includes the concepts of reality and environmental dynamics, which of course all have their part to play within the interpreting setting.

It is felt that this research is important not only to interpreters of British Sign Language, but also to the users of interpreters. If both parties achieve awareness of the influence of self-concepts and biases then this can only benefit all concerned.

LIST OF ABBREVIATIONS

BSL   British Sign Language,

ASL   American Sign Language,

tL   Target Language,

sL   Source Language,

D/deaf Participant   The client that is being interpreted for. In this research a generic "d" has been used in order to reflect the diversity of the client group of the BSL Interpreter.

Hearing Participant   The hearing client that is being interpreted for.

CHAPTER ONE

PSYCHODYNAMIC THEORY AND THE INTER-PRETER

Dynamics in general can be described as:
"The forces that produce change in any field or system".
("Collins Concise" 1995, p.287).
Redfield and Adrienne (1995, p.61) describe these forces in relation to society in the following terms:
"All energy is interconnected, it is malleable to human consciousness through the action of intention. Our radiating thoughts and feelings cause energy to flow out into the world and effect other energy systems".

Figure 1.1 illustrates this concept visually within the context of the interpreting situation. The dynamics portrayed are those of all individuals within the interpreting situation; of the hearing participant, the deaf participant, and also of the influence that the interpreter's dynamics have upon them. It is illustrated at present with only the interpreter's dynamics influencing the other parties, although of course, every individual does have an effect on all parties and this will be examined later. The very fact of a close communication act having a third person present produces an effect.

THE PSYCHODYNAMIC EFFECTS ON THE INTERPRETING PROCESS Figure 1.1

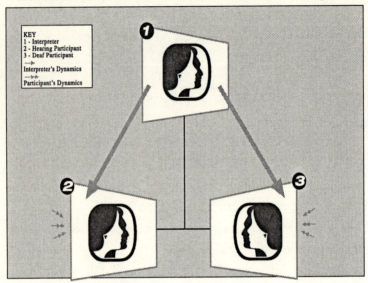

KEY
1 - Interpreter
2 - Hearing Participant
3 - Deaf Participant
----▷ Interpreter's Dynamics
----▷▷ Participant's Dynamics

Freud's psychodynamic theory argues that every individual human mind has an ego, superego and id.

"The ego is concerned with conscious thinking; the id deals with basic motivational forces (e.g. the sexual instinct); and the superego is concerned with moral issues. More specifically, the superego consists of the conscience and the ego-ideal. Our conscious makes us feel ashamed or guilty when we have behaved badly, whereas our ego-ideal makes us feel proud of ourselves when we have behaved well in the face of temptation". (Eysenck 1996, p.172)

To aid comprehension of this theory, Cook (1993, p.115) illustrates how it can be presented via a topographical model of the human mind. (See figure 2.1).

Thus, to Freud the relationship between these three dynamic systems determine each individual's response in communication. It has been acknowledged that this approach to personality has been termed "psychodynamic" since it portrays:

THE PSYCHODYNAMIC EFFECTS ON THE INTERPRETING PROCESS
Figure 2.1: "The Topography of the human mind, according to Freud"
(In Cook 1993, p. 115)

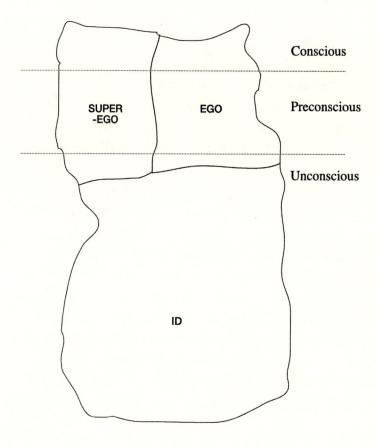

"the ego as keeping a dynamic (constantly changing) balance between the three sets of demands which are on it: those from the id, from the superego and from reality". (Hayes and Orrell 1993, p.228).

If this determines each person's response in communication, then it must also determine the interpreter's response, even if this is at a paralinguistic level; for he or she is also a person. It is important to note that other psychologist's theories do differ from this in part. Fadiman and Frager (1994, p.70) note that Jung, for example, feels that the human mind consists of the persona, as discussed briefly in the introduction, the ego in the conscious, the shadow anima/animus (biased by gender) and the self within the unconscious. He describes the self as:

"the self is more deeply unconscious than the other structures of the personality but at the same time, it is also the centre of the total personality". (Fadiman and Frager, Loc.cit).

If Freud's theory of the three dynamic systems of the human mind is accepted, and also the theory of self concept of every individual, and part of Jung's theory of the persona and the self, it may seem that it is nearly impossible to understand any individual. However, human beings do share similarities. Perhaps one of Jung's most famous findings is that of the concept of archetypes. Stevens elaborates Jung's ideas *"Archetypes are identical psychic structures common to all (GWV, para 224), which together constitute the archaic heritage of humanity"* (CWV, para 259), (Stevens 1994, p.34).

He conceived them to be:

"innate neuropsychic centres possessing the capacity to initiate, control, and mediate the common behavioural characteristics and typical experiences of all human beings. Thus, on appropriate occasions, archetypes give rise to similar thoughts, images, mythologems, feelings and ideas in people, irrespective of their class, creed, race, geographical location, or historical epoch". (Stevens, Op.cit., p.32).

Parker, (1991) refers psychodynamic theory directly to the discourse and the role of language. He argues that reflexivity is the core of human agency and understanding:

"The capacity to be reflexive is the point of connection between the individual and the social". (Parker 1991:105)

This view however is partly challenged by Augoustinos and Walker (1995, p.279) as:

"While the capacity for self-reflection and reflection of others is itself embedded in language and is therefore social and symbolic in nature, it seems to us difficult to deny that reflexivity is, at some level, a cognitive activity".

Freud and Jung both agree that personal and cognitive experience is of crucial significance in the development of the individual's personality and differ only in the fact that Jung:

"denies that this development occurred in an unstructured personality. On the contrary, for Jung the role of

personal experience was to develop what is already there - to activate the archetype potential already present in the Self". (Stevens, Op.cit., p.34).

Although subsequent psychologists have expanded and modified some of these theories, it is sufficient here to summarise that

1. The human mind consists of an ego, superego and id (according to Freud), and the self-concept.
2. The human mind has a self, which is the totality of the personality, and the persona - the mask that the individual presents to the world (according to Jung).
3. Cognitive and personal experience is necessary for the development of the personality.
4. Reflexivity connected to psychodynamic theory is related directly to one's own language and to the understanding of others via cognitive activity.
5. Reflexivity and archetypes make up the shared elements that human beings possess, and aid an understanding and connection between the individual and society in general.
6. Dynamics and thus energy is a constant flow between individuals and is effected by the actions of individuals.

This existing research provides a framework into which the interpreter must now be introduced. The interpreter's role should be to facilitate communication and so it would be helpful first to look at monolingual communication or at how two people communicate without an interpreter. Figure 3.1.1 illustrates this. Here, the sender gives the message via the desired channel, for example, voice, sign or text, and then the receiver retrieves this message, encodes it, comprehends it and then selects the appropriate channel to carry on the conversation, if appropriate.

However, when translating this communication act, as the interpreter is required to do, the process becomes more complex, involving two codes. (See figure 3.1.2). In this instance the interpreter, receives the code, recognises it, decodes it, retrieves it, comprehends it, and then selects code 2, where he/she then encodes the message, selects the channel and transmits. Obviously it can be seen that the translating model of communication involves many more processes than monolingual communication.

The initial message is having to be encoded twice; once in order for the receiver, the interpreter in this case, to understand it and then again for it to be transferred to the appropriate target language. As has been explained, the intention here is not to establish the process of interpreting in itself, nor to establish exactly how this process is carried out. The important element to be focused on is how the interpreter perceives and understands this information. This will affect how it is decoded and whether it is transmitted in the target language, exactly as the speaker required it to be received. In order to expand on this Gerbner's model (1956) could be used. (See Figure 4.1).

"The process begins with an event E, something in external reality which is perceived by M. M's perception of E is a percept E1. This is the perceptual dimension at the start of the process. The relationship between E and E1 involves selection, in that M cannot possibly perceive the whole complexity of E. Human perception is not a simple reception of stimuli, but is a process of interaction or negotiation. What happens is that we try to match the external stimuli with internal patterns of thought or concepts. When this match has been made, we have perceived something, we have given it meaning. So meaning in this sense derives from the matching of external stimuli with internal concepts". (Fiske 1990,p.25).

However, we need to ask where these thoughts and concepts originate from, and how individuals have these internal concepts in order to attribute meaning to received stimuli. It could be suggested that they originate from cognitive information and life experience that the individual has had.

Figure 1.2 gives a visual representation of the concepts discussed so far. As these experiences and the thoughts that they evoke have been produced, so they are stored. These then become experiences and information that the individual can retrieve when required, or may be unexpectedly triggered, which could be fortunate or unfortunate. For ease of comprehension, each individual's cognitive and life experiences have been conceptu-alised as being files held within a filing cabinet so that they can be retrieved when needed. Remember however, these can also be retrieved without authorised recall and emerge from this "filing cabinet". This will be expanded upon later but for now the concept of information storage needs to be concentrated upon.

If the analogy with the filing cabinet is used further though, we need to ascertain how each individual's store of information is kept up to date throughout their life? This is where the domain of schemata becomes apparent.

THE PSYCHODYNAMIC EFFECTS ON THE INTERPRETING PROCESS
Figure 3.1.1: "Monolingual Communication"
(Bell 1991, p. 18)

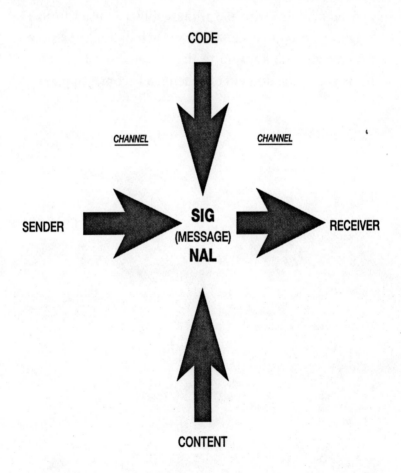

THE PSYCHODYNAMIC EFFECTS ON THE INTERPRETING PROCESS
Figure 3.1.2: "Translating"
(Bell 1991, p. 19)

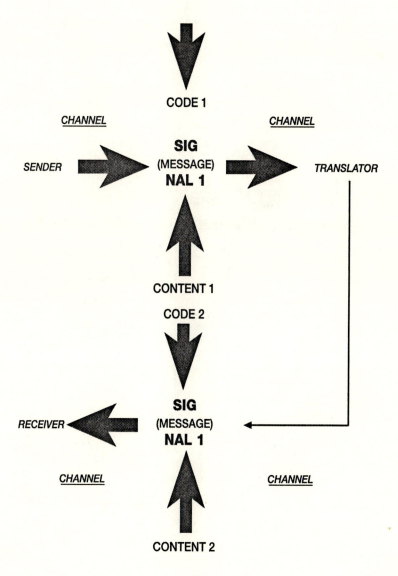

THE PSYCHODYNAMIC EFFECTS ON THE INTERPRETING PROCESS
Figure 4.1: "General Purpose Model of Communication"
Gerbner's Model (1956) In Fiske (1990, p.25)

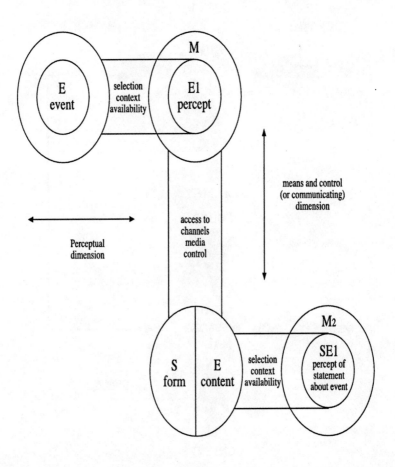

THE PSYCHODYNAMIC EFFECTS ON THE INTERPRETING PROCESS - Figure 1.2

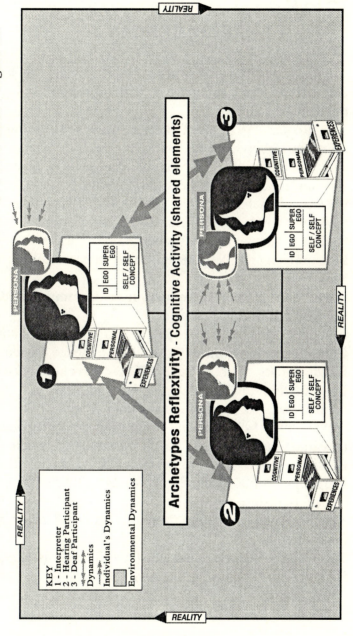

REFERENCES

Augoustinos Martha, Walker Iain, 1995, **"Social Cognition, An Integrated Introduction"**, Sage Publications, London.

Bell Roger, 1991, **"Translation and Translating"**, Longman Group UK Ltd, Essex.

Cook Mark, 1993, **"Levels of Personality, Second Edition"**, Cassell Publishers Ltd, London.

Eysenck Michael, 1996, **"Simply Psychology"**, Psychology Press Publishers, Hove, East Sussex.

Fadiman James, Frager Robert, 1994, **"Personality, Personal Growth"**, Harpercollins College Publishers, New York.

Fiske John, 1990, **"Introduction to Communication Studies"**, Routledge, London.

Gerbner (1956), IN; Fiske John, 1990, **"Introduction to Communication Studies"**, page 25, Routledge, London.

Hayes Nicky, Orrell Sue, 1993, **"Psychology An Introduction"**, Longman Group UK Ltd, London.

Parker 1991:105, as cited Augoustinos Martha.

Walker Iain, 1995, **"Social Cognition An Integrated Introduction"**, page 279, Sage Publications, London.

Redfield James, Carol Adrienne, 1995, **"The Celestine Prophecy. An Experimental Guide"**, 1995, Bantam Books, Berkshire.

Stevens Anthony, 1994, **"Jung"**, Oxford University Press, Oxford.

The Collins Concise Dictionary and Thesaurus, 1995, Harpercollins Publishing, London.

CHAPTER 2

THE UNCONSCIOUS BEING

The Swiss psychologist Piaget established the notion of schemata during his work with children. These findings changed the way psychology viewed cognitive development:

"Upon encountering a novel object or event, the child attempts to understand it in terms or pre-existing schema. (Piaget called this the process of assimilation: the child attempts to assimilate the new event to the pre-existing schema). If the old schema is not adequate to accommodate the new event, then the child - like a good scientist - modifies the schema and thereby extends his or her theory of the world. (Piaget called this the process of accommodation)". (Piaget and Inhelder 1969, p.84).

From this it can be deduced that existing schemas are built up through life experience and cognitive development. As schemas are being updated all the time, other people's experiences will become part of an individual's schema, as their information is told or expressed.

Schemas have three characteristics:
1. Life experience
2. Default valve
3. Other peoples experience

Default valves are devices that come into play where only a limited amount of information is given. The valve is used in order to understand this information from existing schemas. Schemata represent knowledge and have within it subsections:

1. Knowledge
2. Scripts
3. Slots/fillers

The scripts enable a sort of inference to take place. They contain information so that if a person said "I am going shopping", it would be understood, and the speaker would not have to explain every aspect of going shopping; collecting a trolley, walking around the shop and gathering food and so on. Slots and fillers could be described as the words associated with another word. For Example, the word "school" may link to other words such as "teacher". (Dekesel 1996).

It is unnecessary to expand further on Schemata theory but it can be seen that schemata is essential to the interpreter in order for him/her to have the information needed in order to interpret. Without schemata, the interpreter would not understand the most basic of concepts, and thus would not be able to translate them. Figure 1.3 gives a simple illustration of the theory. In Figure 1.2 each individual's cognitive and personal experience was conceptualised as being stored in a filing cabinet, but here, the figure is updated. It now illustrates how schemata, represented as a hand for ease of comprehension, updates the filing cabinet enabling new information and experiences to be entered into the store, and modifies existing files.

The files, therefore, provide each individual with the knowledge that they have acquired throughout their life. If Gerbner's model is now looked at once more, it can be seen that this allows for the external stimuli to correspond to the internal concepts. However, these internal concepts must be within the filing cabinet in order for them to be recalled.

Augoustinos and Walker (1995, p.43) however point out that:

"Information processing is therefore conceptualised as theory driven, rather than data driven; that is, it relies on peoples prior expectations, preconceptions and knowledge about the social world in order to make sense of new situations and encounters. An inherent feature of theory driven or schematic processing is that often it can lead to biased judgements".

Chomsky (1968, p.23) reinforces this by commenting that:

"The person who has acquired knowledge of a language has internalised a system of rules that relate sound and meaning in a particular way".

17

If this is true of a language that utilises sound, it must also be allowed to be true of a language that utilises visual parameters. An interpreter must have acquired knowledge of a language in order to interpret into that language, but we need to consider whether an interpreter of British Sign Language might already have perceived a biased judgement of it?

In a short survey of ten British Sign Language interpreters active within the field, they were asked about the possible varying language levels that could be utilised for each individual when voicing over for a deaf participant, i.e. from British Sign Language to English. Three felt that it depended upon the style presented and the command the participant had of his/her first language. The other seven felt that the English level should be lowered regardless. The latter view does not seem to be reflective of the proficiency of the deaf client's first language level?

Why do these seven interpreters hold this view? When they were questioned further upon these thoughts, the main consensus was that the deaf participants would not have a proficient command of the English language, and that therefore their voice-over should be reflective of the deaf person's English Language. This would seem to be merely transliteration? Indeed translation, which is what the interpreter should be doing, is decoding the linguistic and paralinguistic entities from the Source Language (sL) and producing them within the Target Language (tL), as if all the parties shared the same first language.

Thus, proficiency in the sL should and ought to be reflected in the proficiency of the tL. This is how the sL would be perceived if there was no need for an interpreter. Paradoxically, however, the seven interpreters who said they would lower their English level would be creating a perception for the receiver via a falsified language level and thus the communication would fail.

The interpreters were then asked if they would feel the same way if interpreting for a French client, as naturally a French client's command of the English language, if they were requiring an interpreter, would also not be proficient. In reply to this five said that they had not thought of it that way and that they would indeed not lower the level of English if interpreting for a French client. The remaining two felt that this was a different situation and could not be compared.

This kind of stereotyping of the deaf person by the seven interpreters in this survey would indeed change the effect of the interpreting situation. It is presenting the persona and self of the deaf participant according to the interpreter's schema and biased judgements, rather than according to the individual deaf participant themselves. It must also be noted that the hearing participant's perceptions of the deaf participant, may depend on which view the interpreter holds and whether their voice-over gave the correct and appropriate language level and style and was reflective of the deaf person's proficiency and knowledge.

So why is there this discrepancy? Of the ten interpreters surveyed, the seven interpreters who felt that the language level should be lowered had not been through any interpreter training other than short courses on interpreting and language courses. Maybe here lies one answer. Evans (1989, p.7) suggests that:

"In other words, the subject reasons not with the problem as given, but with a personalised representation of it".

Here the interpreter would be using the English level that the deaf participant has, or indeed presuming the level, rather than be reflecting the level of the sL.

In order to be able to understand the level of the sL and proficiency within it, the interpreter needs to be aware of the shared experiences of deaf people within the Deaf community and hence some of their schematic similarities and those of the language.

For many years British Sign Language has not been accepted as a language and recognition of it as a language in its own right is still being fought for. The oral means of education has been forced upon many deaf children and could be seen as a denial of their language. Kyle and Woll (1985, p.5) write:

"...concerns of all education has been the acquisition of spoken communication as the most acceptable means of interaction, people who are unable to communicate through speech are regarded in some measure as inferior. When they go on to develop their own means of communication, which is usually not that of their parents, then the majority of the community tend to ostracise them

THE PSYCHODYNAMIC EFFECTS ON THE INTERPRETING PROCESS - Figure 1.3

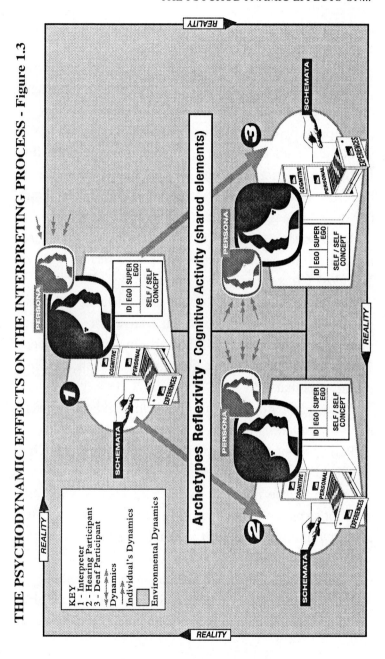

and may ascribe to them levels of competence well below that of the rest of the community".

Although the interpreters in the survey outlined above do indeed accept British Sign Language as a language, are they not sending the subliminal message to hearing participants by devaluing the BSL user's command of the sL because their command of English is not good? If this is so, then oppression is one element that could so easily manifest within the interpreting situation. Baker-Shenk (1986, p.44) suggests that:

"interpreters, by virtue of their 'hearing heritage' and the context in which they work, run a serious risk of behaving in an oppressive manner".

Therefore, it is clear that an understanding of these cross-cultural differences is imperative for the interpreter. An understanding of the participants' self-concept further aids the communication process. Eysenck (1996, p.6) quotes that:

"This neglect of most of the worlds cultures restricts our understanding of human behaviour".

Perhaps one of the most important elements that schemata theory offers for the interpreter is the knowledge that he/she needs to understand his/her own self-concept so as not to portray his/her own schematic influences within the translation and thus bias the interpreting situation.

With knowledge of the participants' cultures and an insight into their experiences the interpreter is more able to understand their message and their self-concept.

He/she can then eliminate negative dynamic effects and instead replace them with positive effects, enabling communication via a tL that is meaningful, reflective of the sL meaning and is understood by all parties - as is the purpose of communication.

"The more we become conscious of ourselves through self knowledge, the more the layer of the personal unconscious that is superimposed on the collected unconscious will be diminished". (Fadiman and Frager 1994, p.81).

The interpreter must have an understanding also of the situation that he/she is entering into. This is important not only for the comprehension of the information he/she will translate, but also for the effects that this situation may have on himself/herself - as an individual with his/her own thoughts, feelings and attitudes towards the information. In other words, they need to be aware that the filing cabinet could fly open at any time. An awareness of the contents of it allows it to be locked, or at least reviewed at a later stage!

To expand on the importance of this, Clore and Gerrod Parrott (1991, p.117) produce a model of conceptions of the mood influence process and introduce theories of "priming" and "mood-as-information" that can interfere and thus influence this situation. (See Figure 5.1). Clore and Gerrod Parrott (Op.cit., p118), explain that:

"Priming is believed to be automatic, to involve the unconscious activation of mood-congruent memories and concepts, and to exert its influence on interpretations

DONNA L. McKENZIE

Figure 5.1: "Conceptions of the mood influence process as depicted by priming and mood-as-information theories"
Clore and Gerrod Parrott (1991, p.117)

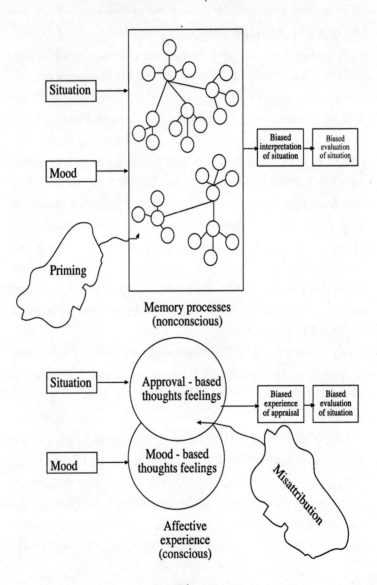

24

of incoming information. By contrast, the processes involved in the mood-as-information hypothesis are believed to involve the conscious experience of mood-related reactions and to depend on implicit attributions about their source".

They believe that the priming hypothesis and mood-as-information hypothesis are related. Their study suggests that human beings carry out an appraisal of the external situation and their interpretation of the stimuli that are received could be influenced heavily by the person's mood/emotion and their cognitive priming (even with non-emotional information). They suggest, therefore, that the interpretation does not stem directly from the stimuli or the information itself. There are also "self-triggers" (information and past experience perhaps hidden so deeply that not even the individual knows of its existence until it provokes an unexpected emotive response).

The concepts of the internal and external monitor (Steiner 1997), become crucial here and the interpreter should address them at all times. Thus, the interpreter should always be aware of the environment and the responses of the tL audience via the external monitor. They should also be introspectively monitoring themselves in order to evaluate the coherence of the language being produced and the message being portrayed. This is vitally important if the content of the given scenario is provoking unexplained emotive responses within the interpreter, even at a paralinguistic level, altering the speaker's intent and persona.

These unconscious and conscious attributions or 'cognitive feelings' are however not all negative and are important and relevant to every individual's relationship to events and information. As Clore and Gerrod Parrott, (Op.cit., p.108) comment:

"We are informed about the significance of events by our own affective reactions to them.....such emotional experiences serve as information for judgement and decision-making processes".

This could relate to some extent to the 'default valve' discussed earlier in the theory of schemata. The emotion and mood that is evoked acts as additional information, and enables the individual to relate to the external stimuli.

All the theories looked at in this chapter emphasise the individuality of every human being - including the interpreter. One concept stimulus will ignite many concepts and emotions in each person. The important element therefore that the interpreter has to be aware of, is that although these emotions act as additional information, they also have the potential to influence the sL message when translating into the tL.

The default valve is a very important tool that the interpreter has, and the greater the experience and world knowledge that the interpreter possesses, the more resources he/she has available when portraying the sL. Thus, the sL is understood precisely and proficiently and decoded, analysed and produced within the tL maintaining the intent of the speaker and the correct perception by the tL audience is achieved. If the culture and sL is not understood, it cannot be translated into the tL. It is merely transliterated. Where transliteration rather than translation occurs, the appropriate language level has not been sought, nor has the intent or persona of the sL speaker been preserved. In order for true translation to be carried out impartially the interpreter also has to be aware of their own unconscious elements that are at work within the decoding and encoding of language. Although these elements are necessary for understanding, they have a potential of changing the intended message of the speaker.

When there is an awareness of these elements by the interpreter, their essence can be brought to the conscious level by the very knowledge of their existence, and be understood and controlled. Thus, in other words, the interpreter can utilise cognition as a tool.

REFERENCES

Augoustinos Martha, Walker Iain, 1995, **"Social Cognition, An Integrated Introduction"**, Sage Publications, London.

Baker-Shenk Charlotte, 1986, **"The Characteristics of Oppressed and Oppressor Peoples: Their Effect on the Interpreting Context"**, p44, IN McIntire L Marina (Ed), 1986.

"Interpreting: The Art of Cross Cultural Mediation. Proceedings of the Ninth National Convention of the Registry if Interpreters for the Deaf July 4 - 8, 1985", RID Publications, Silver Spring, United States of America.

Chomsky Noam, 1968, **"Language and Mind"**, Harcourt, Brace and World Inc, London.

Clore L Gerald, Parrott Gerrod W, 1991, **"Moods and Their Vicissitudes: Thoughts and Feelings as Information"**, IN; Forgas P Joseph, 1991, **"Emotion and Social Judgement"**, Pergamon Press, Oxford.

Dekesel K, 18/11/96, **Lecture notes,** Wolverhampton.

Evans, St. B.T. Johnathon, 1989, **"Bias in Human Reasoning, Causes and Consequences"**, Lawrence Erlbaum Associates, Hove, East Sussex.

Eysenck Michael, 1996, **"Simply Psychology"**, Psychology Press Publishers, Hove, East Sussex.

Fadiman James, Frager Robert, 1994, **"Personality, Personal Growth"**, Harpercollins College Publishers, New York.

Kyle G, Woll B, 1985, **"Sign Language The Study of**

Deaf People and Their Language", Cambridge University Press, Northamptonshire.

Piaget and Inhelder, 1969, IN; Aitchison L Rita, Aitchison G, Richardson, Smith, E Edward, Ben L Daryl, 1993, **"Introduction to Psychology Eleventh Edition",** Ted Buchhols,

Steiner B, 1997, **Lecture Notes,** Wolverhampton,

With thanks to the participants who kindly agreed to take part in the research presented within this chapter. Their names will remain anonymous, as is their wishes. Interviews took place in London during February 1997.

CHAPTER 3

COGNITION AS A TOOL

In the translation process, cognition can be utilised as a tool only with comprehension of and also with an understanding of the cognitive and cultural experiences of the sL and tL groups. In the case of British Sign Language interpreting, the Deaf community and its members are perhaps the more important client group to concentrate on.

Within chapter two it has been suggested that many deaf people's cognitive experience has been affected by the oppression from hearing people, be that from society as a whole, or at a young age from the education system which may have put the need to speak above the need to communicate[2]

---

2 Throughout this research this aspect of deaf education has been briefly touched upon. For more information on this please refer to Kyle and Woll, 1985, "Sign Language The Study of Deaf People and Their Language", p37 - 58 and p230 - 242.

It is not surprising then that an interpreter from this hearing community may be viewed by the deaf person negatively. It should also be noted that the code of conduct for spoken language interpreters dictates that the only language they shall interpret into is their mother tongue, or language of habitual use. (Institute of Linguists, 1998). However, unless a British Sign Language interpreter has deaf parents, and thus their first language is British Sign Language, the majority of BSL interpreters will be interpreting into their second language.

British Sign Language is a visual language, and thus to begin this chapter about the understanding and utilising of cognition, the working of the brain needs to be considered. Different parts of the brain have different functions. In simple terms, the right cortex of the brain is responsible for rhythm, spatial awareness, gestalt (whole picture), imagination, daydreaming, colour, and dimension. The left cortex is responsible for words, logic, numbers, sequence, linearity, analysis and lists. (Buzan 1997, p.18). From this information it could be ascertained that a person conversing in spoken English would use the language (left cortex) part of the brain, while a person conversing using British Sign Language (a visual language) would be using the right side of the brain. However, findings by neurologists of ASL users that have been brain damaged suggest otherwise.

"There exist right-hemisphere deficits that impair one's understanding of space, typically producing a so-

called left neglect. People with these deficits fail to see things in the left half of their visual field....but if they happen to be ASL speakers, they still use the left side of the space in front of them just for the purpose of signing ASL syntax. Another kind of right hemisphere damage can lead to loss of the ability to produce facial expressions, but despite such damage, ASL speakers can produce facial expressions that are relevant to ASL grammar, using the very same muscles". (Jackendoff 1993, p.151).

This, Jackendoff argues, proves that:

"ASL is a language, not a collection of pantomimes and facial expressions. And is localised in the language areas of the brain, in a different place from pantomimes and facial expressions".

Not only do these findings provide even further evidence to support the argument that sign languages are indeed languages, they also suggest that language is not purely left-sided or right-sided in its origins or its perception. Jackendoff further suggests that the construction of experience and the internalisation of mental grammar allows language to be produced and understood.

"Our experience and understanding of stimuli in each domain is actively constructed by our minds, making essential use of the abstract mental patterns specific to that domain". (Jackendoff Op.cit., p179).

In other words, each person's internalised mental grammar is built up through personal and cognitive experiences, which stimulate the brain to allow interpretation of language and patterns within the world. To sum this up, Buzan (Op.cit., p19) comments that:

"It seems, then, that when we describe ourselves as talented in certain areas and not talented in others, what we are really describing is those areas of our potential that we have successfully developed, and those areas of our potential that still lie dormant, which in reality could, with the right nurturing, flourish".

Therefore, the mental grammar of an interpreter whose first language is spoken English will differ from that of a person whose first language is a visual language.

This is because their cognitive experience is through English, and patterning for their language is linear. The person with a visual language will have a pattern recognition via visual as opposed to linear parameters. This has an effect for the interpreter who is portraying a concept. For if the tL group is the Deaf Community, the tL must be aligned with the internalised mental grammar of this group, in order for full comprehension to be achieved. Thus, the tL must be language produced visually, matching the internalised grammar of the tL audience, just as it would be if it were the mother tongue of the BSL interpreter. It must not be a linear attempt of English in sign. McIntire (1986, p.51) comments that:

"It is fair to say that the majority of hearing people who work as "interpreters" are far from fluent..and that most of them transliterate rather than interpret...then simply don't use signs for English words such as 'is', 'are' and past tense '-ed"'.

Marc Marschark (1998) reiterates the importance of matching cognitive structures, and language patterns of individuals in his research into mental representation and memory of deaf adults and children. He suggests that finger spelling is perceived as a speech skill rather than a sign skill. Although it can be found within BSL grammar, he suggests it is not representative of the internalised grammar or cognitive structures of the users of that language:

"The demonstration that digit span is positively related to speech skill and negatively to sign skill among deaf students also points to the importance of structuring both laboratory tasks and classroom situations in ways that appropriately map onto student's cognitive structures. We need to distinguish possible effects due to linguistic coding per se". (Marschark, Op.cit., p16/17).

This research illustrates to the interpreter the importance of matching the cognitive structures and linguistic coding via internalised mental grammar of the tL audience, and also the importance of paying adequate attention to training for interpreters in order for them to appreciate the tL audience's cognitive experiences, if they have not already acquired them through natural childhood language acquisition.[3] Interpreters need to have this understanding, both linguistic and cultural, if they are to have the same level of understanding that a spoken language interpreter would have when they are interpreting into their own mother tongue. This also emphasises the fact that the spoken language interpreter would share common experiences with their client group in a way that most BSL interpreters (with the exception of first language users of BSL) would not share with theirs.[4]

Furthermore, even if their first language is BSL, they will not have shared the exact experiences with their client group because they are not deaf.

Enculturisation, it could be argued, is perhaps the only way to acquire this internalised mental grammar, although this raises a further dilemma for the BSL interpreter, because deaf people will have differing internalised mental grammars.

This will have arisen because of differences in education, home life, choice or acquisition of language variation and register and the fact that BSL has not been standardised unlike English, French and many, if not all other spoken languages.

Despite all this however, visual perception and an understanding of internalised mental processes of the visual language are of utmost importance; and they are important issues relating to both comprehension and production. The deaf participant needs to understand the production of the interpreter and needs the interpreter to understand his/her production. Comprehension and production are also of relevance for the hearing participant because if the deaf participant does not understand the interpreter's production then the hearing person's questions will not be fully understood, and communication will break down. Training is of importance here in order for the interpreter to be able to ascertain the correct register to use in order to produce cohesion within the tL.

This training is also of optimum importance in order for the BSL interpreter to acquire the appropriate internalised mental grammar in a visual capacity, because it will have first been acquired by them in its acoustic representation. This acquisition serves to meet the needs of the client group in cultural and cognitive understanding, and once more stresses the issue of cross-cultural mediation.[5]

All that has so far been discussed about cognition as a tool also relates to the linguistic relativity hypothesis.

"The linguistic relativity hypothesis suggests that our language affects the way that we see the world and that by looking at a language we can come to some understanding of a particular culture". (Hayes and Orrell 1993, p.167). Figure 1.4 adds a final update to the visual representations of the concepts discussed. It incorporates Clore and Gerrod Parrott's (Loc.cit) theories of cognitive priming and mood/emotion-as-information and the importance of internalised mental grammar, and its interconnection with each individual's cognitive experiences especially regarding language.

It should be noted that in Figure 1.4, only the interpreter's mood/emotion and cognitive priming are shown. Of course, each participant does have these elements but here only the interpreter's are shown because of the disasterous effects that can be produced if their own mood/emotion is portrayed instead of that of the intent of the speaker. The other participants are free to allow their mood/emotions to influence the communication as they wish, for it is their discourse.

The interpreter can utilise these elements as a means of additional information in order to relate to the stimuli, but he/she must allow the participants to make their own judgements by transferring the information just as he/she receives it, and not influenced by his/her own cognitive priming or mood/emotion.

In brief therefore, the interpreter must not only understand the language of the client group, but also the culture and their shared cognitive experiences in order to understand fully the people of that language, and in order to translate that language for full comprehension. With this awareness, cognition belonging to both the client groups and that of the interpreter, can be utilised as a tool to aid the communication process.

---

3. This also gives rise to the debate of the needs of deaf children within education, and that this should match the findings of this research. However this is not the subject of this research, and thus will not be addressed. For more information on this please refer to Yule 1996, "The Study of Language, Second Edition", p202 - 213.

4. It must be noted that even with the BSL interpreter who has acquired British Sign Language as their first language, the experience of deafness would not be shared, for the very reason that they themselves are hearing. Perhaps it could be ascertained that a deep understanding of their parent's experiences is held by them, but it cannot be the same as having the experience oneself, first hand. For a deeper insight into this issue please refer to Muggett-DeCaro 1996, "On Being Both Hearing and Deaf: My Bilingual-Bicultural Experience", IN Parasnis (Ed), 1996, "Cultural and Language Diversity and the Deaf Experience", p272 - 289.

5. As has been stated previously, the deaf individuals are thought to be those that identify themselves with the Deaf community, in that British Sign Language is their first or preferred language, and have been deaf from birth, or a young age, in that they have no acoustic memory. It must be noted however, that many members of this community have become deaf at a later stage and thus do have some acoustic memory. For information relating to degrees of hearing loss please refer to Martin and Grover, 1990, "Ears and Hearing", p15 - 41.

DONNA L. McKENZIE

THE PSYCHODYNAMIC EFFECTS ON THE INTERPRETING PROCESS - Figure 1.4

KEY
1 - Interpreter
2 - Hearing Participant
3 - Deaf Participant
Dynamics
Individual's Dynamics
Environmental Dynamics

INFORMATION

Mood / Emotion
cognitive priming

Archetypes Reflexivity - Cognitive Activity (shared elements)

REALITY

REFERENCES

Buzan Tony, 1997, **"Use Your Head"**, BBC Books, London.

Hayes Nicky, Orrell Sue, 1993, **"Psychology. An Introduction"**, Longman Group UK Ltd, London,

Institute of Linguists, 1998, **"Code of Professional Conduct"**, London.

Jackendoff Ray, 1993, **"Patterns In the Mind, Language and Human Nature"**, Harvester Wheatsheaf, Hemel Hempstead, Hertfordshire.

Marschark Marc, 1998, **"Mental Representation and Memory in Deaf Adults and Children"**, Rochester Institute of Technology, New York.

Martin Michael, Grover Brian, 1990, **"Ears and Hearing"**, Macdonald and Co Publishers Ltd, London,

McIntire L Marina (Ed), 1986, **"Interpreting: The Art of Cross Cultural Mediation, proceedings of the Ninth National Convention of the Registry of Interpreters for the Deaf July 4 - 8 1985"**, RID Publications, Silver Spring, United States of America.

Parasnis Ila (Ed), 1996, **"Cultural and Language Diversity and the Deaf Experience"**, Cambridge University Press, United States of America,.Yule George, 1996, **"The Study of Language, Second Edition"**, Cambridge University Press, Cambridge.

CHAPTER 4

INTROSPECTIVE RESEARCH

Methodology Implemented

This research looks at the psychodynamic effects on the interpreting process which obviously involves the mental states that can, and may well, influence a situation.

Introspective research was, therefore, felt to be the most appropriate method to implement. Gellatly (1986, p.7) suggests that introspection is done by *"..asking other people about their observations of their minds at work, that is by collecting reports of their introspections. Certainly introspection is an important and frequently used method of studying the mind"*.

Four groups of people were targeted:
1.   Interpreters of spoken language
2.   Interpreters of BSL
3.   Hearing participants who had used a spoken lan guage interpreter
4.   Deaf participants who had used a BSL interpreter

Ten representatives of each of the four groups took part in this research. The format and delivery of the questionnaires was arrived at by considering the results of a pilot study done at the start of the research. Three questionnaires were designed in order to make sure that the questions asked were the same for each group of participants.

The same questionnaire was given to spoken language and BSL interpreters, and two separate questionnaires were given to the hearing and deaf participants in order that their levels of comprehension should not bias the results, nor that their English be tested in any way.

The questionnaire for deaf participants was designed so that further information could be obtained about the deaf participants' schooling. This served to clarify when BSL was acquired, what type of schooling they had had, (for example oral, total communication, Deaf school and so on). Having the two questionnaires also allowed for culturally specific questions to be asked, such as how much the participants connected themselves to their communities etc, enabling clearer and more precise results to be obtained.

Although variables such as age and gender of each individual are noted within figure 6.2, no control study was done, and a larger research study would need to be carried out in order to gain an insight into whether variables of this kind are relevant factors. Most of the questionnaires were presented in a one-to-one interview in order for all questions to be fully understood, and for the researcher to ask for points to be expanded upon if necessary. However, where geographical location or the availability of the participant made this not possible, the questionnaires were distributed by post.

In this case, a covering letter fully explained the reason for the questionnaire, and contact details were given in case any of the questions where not fully understood. All participants were asked to give as detailed an answer as they could. It should be noted that when hearing participants that used a spoken language interpreter were interviewed, a member of that community would be briefed on the questions and they then conducted the interview.

This method ensured that the results would not be influenced by unwanted dynamics associated with a researcher who did not originate from or participate in that community. It was acknowledged that if the person conducting the interview shared a mutual aim or identity with the participant it enabled the interviewee to 'introspect' with more ease, and not worry that there was a 'right' or 'wrong' answer.

Although this research focused on the deaf participants that use BSL/English interpreters, it must not be forgotten that hearing participants also use this interpreter. It is a myth that only a deaf person needs an interpreter, but for this research the findings from the hearing participants were not expanded upon as no real dilemmas were noted by them, except that at first they found it strange and sometimes an intrusion to use an interpreter. However, it could be another interesting research topic to look at why hearing participants and deaf participants differ so much in their perception of the interpreting situation, and how that relates to the reality of their experience.

A note is perhaps required here as to why spoken language interpreters, and also hearing participants who had used a spoken language interpreter, were incorporated into this research. This was done in order to find out if the attitudes of both the interpreters and participants differed from those of the BSL interpreters and deaf participants. If this was found to be the case, then it would emphasise the importance of cultural and cognitive factors, particularly in the BSL interpreting model.

Of the ten spoken languages interpreters five had obtained further or higher qualifications for interpreting, and five had no further qualifications, other than that the language that they interpreted into was their mother tongue. This is referred to as 'mother tongue training'. Of the BSL interpreters, five had degree level studies associated with interpreting (Graduate Interpreters) or had become Council for the Advancement of Communication with Deaf People (CACDP) registered qualified interpreters, and five had language qualifications up to CACDP Stage two, and a communicating qualification. This spectrum was taken to reflect the reality of individuals actively working within the field as interpreters. Figure 6.1 represents this information.

The results of the introspective research were most inform-
ative, but perhaps the most relevant were the results to questions relating to oppression/dynamic effects and cultural
awareness and mediation. When asked to discuss the factors of
oppression and dynamic effects upon the interpreting situation, the following results emerged:

Eight of the ten spoken language interpreters thought that
the presence of an interpreter did not have any adverse effect,
but indeed made the situation more positive, and gave the
client confidence. Of the two interpreters that did feel an effect
was evident, one had been educated to degree level (the only
spoken language interpreter in this research that had received
a degree), and the other had acquired the majority of her interpreting skills through mother tongue training and one communicating qualification.

The main reason for her answer was her knowledge from
observing other interpreters. All of the BSL interpreters that
had acquired or were acquiring degree level qualifications for
interpreting (Graduate Interpreters), or were registered with
CACDP, felt that having an interpreter there did have an effect
upon the situation, apart from one who felt no effect was evident. The interpreters that had communicating qualifications
or language qualifications felt that no such effects were evident, apart from one who had been working in the field for
more than ten years.

These results suggest that the training that these interpreters
have received has a direct effect upon their ability to introspect
upon their work, and upon the knowledge that an interpreter's
presence can have an effect. They also suggest that the experience that the individual possesses, and the insight that this provides has an implication. Responses as to how, and indeed if,
cultural transferral and understanding were felt to be relevant
for the interpreter reinforced these findings.

Seven of the spoken language interpreters felt that comprehension and meaning were the most important elements. The remaining three felt that literal word for word rendition of the sL was the important element, and it was their role to provide this. Of these three, none had received further training, apart from having the language as their mother tongue.

This illustrates that perhaps 'mother tongue training' in complex interpreting assignments is not enough for interpreters, and that further training is required to gain knowledge of possible effects produced by the interpreter, and knowledge of how to translate in order to aid comprehension by the client group. A similar split in results appeared within the BSL interpreters. Seven felt that meaning and comprehension were imperative, whilst three felt a literal word-for-word rendition was appropriate.

It is interesting to note that the three interpreters who felt this had only received communicating qualifications that do not delve into interpreting issues. A comparison of the three interpreters discussed above, and the three 'mother tongue' trained interpreters could be made in relation to the depth of their knowledge of interpreting issues. A further comparison could be made of the answers from trained interpreters of both spoken languages and BSL.

Differences were also apparent between each interpreting group in the qualities and vital elements that they thought were necessary. In the spoken language group the consensus was that knowledge of language and culture, mental resilience and being free of prejudices were imperative. Within the BSL interpreter group there was not a consensus. Many felt that a sense of humour was an important element and also confidentiality.

Fig 6.1 Introspective Research Findings: Interpreter Groups Utilised Within Research

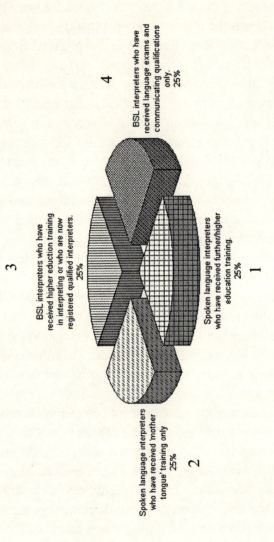

3

BSL interpreters who have
received higher eduction training
in interpreting or who are now
registered qualified interpreters.
25%

4

BSL interpreters who have
received language exams and
communicating qualifications
only.
25%

1

Spoken language interpreters
who have received further/higher
education training.
25%

2

Spoken language interpreters
who have received 'mother
tongue' training only
25%

46

Fig 6.1.1 Introspective research findings : Interpreter Groups

Fig 6.2 Introspective Research Findings : Client Groups

All socialised and identify with the Deaf community.
All attend residential schools.

All educated in respective preferred/first languages.

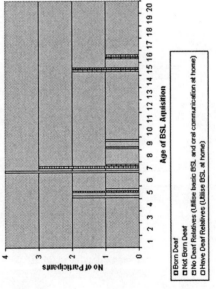

Deaf Participants

No of Participants

Age of BSL Aquisition

☐ Born Deaf
☐ Not Born Deaf
☐ No Deaf Relatives (Utilise basic BSL and oral communication at home)
☐ Have Deaf Relatives (Utilise BSL at home)

Hearing participants

No of Participants

☒ Both parents shared native first language with minimal English skills
■ One parent fluent in first (native) language other parent fluent in English
■ Spoke (first) native language at home
☐ Spoke both first language and English at home

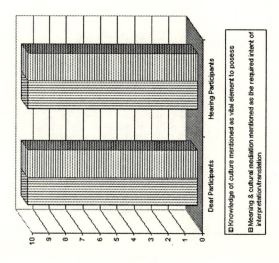

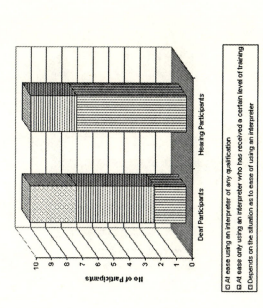

Fig 6.2.2 Introspective Research Findings : Client Groups

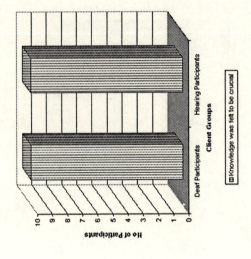

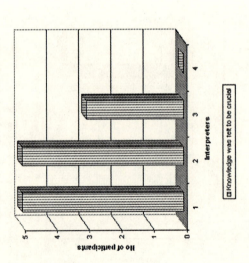

Fig 6.3 Comparison of Introspective Research Findings re. Interpreter and Client Groups

Comparison of Individuals Responses to the Importance of Knowledge of Both Cultures for the Interpreter

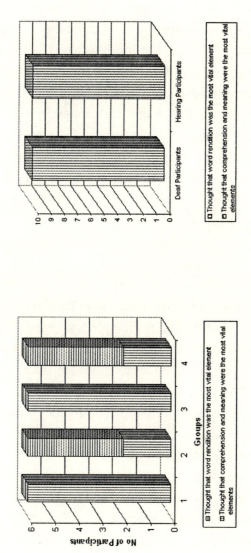

Fig 6.3.1 Comparison of Introspective Research Findings re. Interpreter and Client Groups

Comparism of individuals responses as to the importance of comprehension and meaning being the most vital element in interpreting/translation

However, many responses referred to dress code, and there was no reference to knowledge of cultural or linguistic variations, only a reference to language ability. These results are represented in figure 6.1.1.

It was felt that perhaps the most significant findings from all groups related to what could be termed 'the interpreter's role'. For this reason and for ease of comparison of all groups, figures 6.3 and 6.3.1 were compiled. These show a comparison of the research findings from all groups with regards to the importance of cultural awareness and meaning, and comprehension as opposed to word-for-word rendition.

As can be seen, all of the spoken language interpreters, regardless of their interpreting qualifications, felt that knowledge of culture and mediation were essential. Of the BSL interpreters who had received language and communicating training only, none felt this was of importance. Of those who were registered qualified with CACDP, or who were graduate interpreters, only three felt this was of vital importance.

When this is compared to the expectations of both deaf and hearing participants, a dynamic in itself is apparent, as all twenty felt this to be of optimum importance. With regards to comprehension and meaning, the client groups all felt that this was the most important aspect of interpreting, and in the interview felt that cultural transferral was directly connected to this.

Within the interpreting groups all of the spoken language interpreters that had received further/higher education agreed that comprehension and meaning were vital, apart from one individual. Of the mother tongue trained spoken language interpreters two felt this was important, and three did not. Of the BSL interpreters who were graduates or CACDP qualified, all apart from one felt that comprehension and meaning were imperative, and of the BSL interpreters who had only received language and communicating qualifications only two agreed that comprehension and meaning were vital, and three did not.

REFERENCES

Gellatly Angus (Ed), 1986, **"The Skilful Mind. An Introduction to Cognitive Psychology",** Open University Press, Milton Keynes,

With thanks to the participants within all four groups who kindly agreed to take part within this research study. Their names will remain anonymous as is their wishes.

Interviews took place in London between March 1997 and January 1998, (this is with the inclusion of the questionnaires that had to be posted out).

Chapter 5

CONCLUSION

Interpreting in general has been described as:
"...probably the most complex type of event yet produced in the evolution of the cosmos". (Richards 1953: 250).

Indeed, if this is true, and if the findings from this research are taken into consideration then perhaps it is even more true of BSL/English interpreting. From the outset dynamics were discussed and the theory of psychodynamics. The self concept, schematic influences, cognition, mental grammar and the plasticity of the brain have all been analysed. The importance of bringing these elements from the unconscious to the conscious, so that they can be utilised by the interpreter, has been stressed. Only with this understanding can the interpreter excel in his or her profession, enhancing communication and eliminating unwanted dynamic effects.

Enculturalisation within a community and the acquisition of its language is essential. However, it has been shown by the introspective research study that this alone does not enable an individual to be a successful interpreter. Indeed the research has shown that interpreters do need appropriate training in order for them to realise the potential dilemmas and problems that can arise from their involvement within a situation. What enculturalisation does provide, it would seem, is acceptance within that community by its members. It also gives an individual a depth of understanding of the importance of culture and that culture is indeed embedded within language.

The results show that in most cases spoken language interpreters within this study felt that knowledge and mediation of culture between two languages, and comprehension and meaning are very closely related. The client group also felt the same and expected their interpreters to have that knowledge. Interpreter training programmes at higher education levels allow an individual an insight into the importance of culture, but the spoken language interpreters in the survey did not feel that cultural training was required in order for them to understand the importance of culture; suggesting perhaps that it is inborn.

It can also be seen that the clients of spoken language interpreters are more at ease in using an interpreter, and do not have the same concerns about the level of training that their interpreter has received. This is a very different finding from that of the deaf participants, most of whom wanted an interpreter who has received a certain level of training. Perhaps this is because most BSL interpreters are hearing, and even when they come from a deaf family, they have not themselves been through the same experiences of oppression, difficulties within schooling or the same barriers faced by their deaf peers within everyday life; although it must be noted that they too will have faced this to some extent[6] Being hearing, the BSL interpreter, it must also be remembered, comes from the very community that has created the oppression faced by deaf individuals, and perhaps this too accounts for some differences between the clients of the spoken language and sign language interpreters in these research findings.

This may also explain to some extent why hearing participants using a BSL interpreter felt that they faced no difficulties or dilemmas.

In this way the BSL interpreter must not only be aware of the psychodynamic issues, but also of the fact that for the majority of them the natural acquisition through birth, and indeed the identity of deafness, is one that is not physically shared with the client group. Even if individuals have been born into deaf families they do not share deafness, only a shared perception of it - a problem that does not exist for the spoken language interpreter.

---

[6] During liaisons with hearing individuals of deaf families it has been noted that they very much felt the oppression and barriers that their family members faced. It is the object of this research however to impart that although this is noted, being that they are not deaf themselves this prejudice is different, and the communication barriers faced are therefore different.

Perhaps if the spoken language interpreter did not share their cultural identity with the client group then research findings would be very different, and perhaps this lends itself to a separate research study. Maybe in this way BSL interpreters have to prove their membership, validity and intentions, in order to be accepted into the Deaf Community. They must enculturise themselves.

However, this alone is not enough; neither it would seem is the mere fact of natural acquisition when the profession of interpreting is entered into. Training is still required in order to learn how to translate, how to preserve the intent and persona of each person. That is not acquired through language acquisition alone and is an important notion to reinforce. Even with the research findings here of spoken language interpreters, it must be remembered that language acquisition alone would not allow them to translate/interpret in a professional capacity.

The findings here merely emphasised how their client group perceived them, not the qualifications required in order for them to interpret, although of course on occasion, as in every culture friends and colleagues are asked to assist if they have an understanding of both languages. However in a professional capacity these spoken language interpreters acquire the languages and then obtain degree status in order to translate. Surely this should also be the case for BSL interpreters. Why should deaf (and hearing clients) receive any less?

BSL interpreters must acknowledge the importance of

the notion of the self-concept in relation to their own introspection, their value judgements of others, and the implications in their linguistic evaluation. Even with this in mind, the BSL interpreter must appreciate the complexity and continual flow of dynamic effects within any situation; and remember that while the dynamic elements can assist the process of interpreting, they can also destroy it. If these issues are acknowledged and addressed they can be utilised to the interpreter's advantage; if ignored they can circulate with even more destructive potential. Dollard and Miller (1950, p3) explain the psychotherapeutic situation as providing a kind of window to mental life: *"Advanced research students in psychology are taught the rudiments of the therapist's art so that they may sit at this window"*. This could also be said of the interpreting situation.

An individual is given language and so may enter the room. The culture of that language is embedded all around, and even if one has not grown up within this particular room, if they stay there for a long period of time will become enculturised within it, understand it, perhaps even value its beauty. With training in such skills as interpreting and translation issues, he/she can venture toward the window. This is conceptualised in figure 7.1 as a triangular window, as three is the smallest possible number of participants within an interpreting situation, i.e. initiator of communication, receiver and interpreter.

With understanding of the dynamic effects that the role of the interpreter can bring he/she can unlock and open the window. Only with this window opened can communication with another party be undertaken and thus translated/interpreted. Alternatively, it can remain shut and then a 'false' communication takes place and many factors intrude; the most obvious being the difficulty in hearing or seeing the person on the other side of the window. In this case, perhaps the interpreter changes the words to hide that he or she cannot hear or see them well, and perhaps the person he or she is interpreting for in the room does not notice, for he or she is the interpreter after all.

Rightly or wrongly the interpreting role attracts a status, a 'power' that means he or she can choose whether they open the window, or by leaving it shut they can fail to interpret fully accurately and no-one may know. The choice is yours - as an interpreter. It should not be, but unfortunately that is the status that goes with the role of any interpreter. But is it fair and right for the people both sides of the window? (See Figure 7.1)

REFERENCES

Dollard John, Miller E Neal, 1950, **"Personality and Psychotherapy. An Analysis In Terms of Learning. Thinking and Culture",** McGraw Hill Book Company Inc, United States of America.

Richards, 1953:250 IN Cokely Dennis 1992, **"Interpretation: A Sociolinguistic Model",** Linstock Press, Burtonsville.

THE PSYCHODYNAMIC EFFECTS ON THE INTERPRETING PROCESS - Figure 7.1

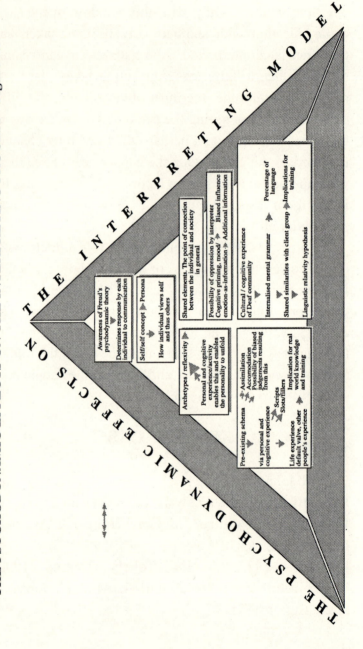

BIBLIOGRAPHY

Adams Parveen (Ed), 1973, **"Language in Thinking"**, Penguin Education, Division of Penguin Books Inc, Harmondsworth.

Ahlgren Inger, Bergman, Brennan Mary (Eds), 1994, **"Perspectives on Sign Language Usage, Salamanca, Spain 25-30 May 1992"**, International Sign Linguistics Association, Durham.

Aitchison L Rita, Aitchison G, Richardson, Smith, Edward E, Ben L Daryl, 1993, **"Introduction to Psychology, Eleventh Edition"**, Ted Buchhols.

Arnold John, Robertson T Ivan, Cooper L Cary, 1991, **"Work Psychology, Understanding Human Behaviour in the Workplace"**, Longman Group UK Ltd, London.

Augoustinos Martha, Walker Iain, 1995, **"Social Cognition, An Integrated Introduction"**, Sage Publications, London

Bell Judith, 1997, **"Doing Your Research Project, Second Edition"**, Open University Press, Buckingham.

Bell Roger T, 1991, **"Translation and Translating"**, Longman Group UK Ltd, Essex.

Berne Eric, 1975, **"Transactional Analysis in Psychotherapy"**, Souvenir Press Ltd, London.

Berne Eric, 1964, **"Games People Play, The Psychology of Human Relationships"**, Penguin Books, London.

Bonnes Mirilia, Secchiardi Giarifranco, 1995,

"Environmental Psychology, A Psycho-social Introduction", Sage Publications, London

Brannan Julia (Ed), 1992, **"Mixing Methods: Qualitative and Quantitative Research"**, Ashgate Publishing Limited, Aldershot.

Brewer B Marilyn, Crano D William, 1994, **"Social Psychology"**, West Publishing Company, Minneapolis.

Brown JAC, 1961, **"Freud and the Post-Freudians"**, Penguin Books Ltd, Middlesex,

Buzan Tony, 1974, **"Use Your Head"**, BBC Books, London.

Cartwright Dorwin, Zander Alvin (Ed), 1968, **"Group Dynamics Research and Theory, Third Edition"**, Tavistock Publications Ltd, London.

Chapman J Anthony, Gale Anthony, 1982, **"Psychology and People. A Tutorial Text"**, British Psychological Society and Macmillan Education Limited, London.

Cheshire M Neil, 1975, **"The Nature of Psychodynamic Interpretation"**, John Wiley and Sons, London.

Chomsky Noam, 1968, **"Language and Mind"**, Harcourt, Brace and World Inc, London.

Cokely Dennis, 1992, **"Interpretation: A Sociolinguistic Model"**, Linstok Press, Burtonsville.

Collins Concise Dictionary and Thesaurus, 1995, Harpercollins Publishers, London.

Cook Mark, 1993, **"Levels of Personality, Second Edition"**, Cassell Publishers Ltd, London,

Corker Mairian, 1990, **"Deaf Perspectives on Psychology,**

Language and Communication Part 1: Experience, Part 2: Self and Identity, Part 3: Psycholinguistics, Part 4: Sociolinguistics, Part 5: Intervention, Part 6: Systems", National Association for Tertiary Education for Deaf People, Sheffield.

De Bono Edward, 1982, **"De Bono's Thinking Course"**, BBC Books, London.

Dekesel K, 1996/7, **Lecture Notes,** Wolverhampton.

Deuchar Margaret, 1984, **"British Sign Language"**, Routledge and Kegan Paul plc, London,

Dewald A Paul, 1964, **"Psychotherapy A Dynamic Approach. Second Edition"**, Blackwell Scientific Publications, Oxford London.

Dollard John, Miller E Neal, 1950, **"Personality and Psychotherapy. An Analysis in Terms of Learning, Thinking and Culture"**, McGraw-Hill Book Company Inc, United States of America.

Duck Steve, 1988, **"Relating to Others"**, Open University Press, Milton Keynes.

Erikson Erik, 1977, **"Childhood and Society"**, Collins Publishing Group, Hove, East Sussex.

Evans St. B.T. Jonathon, 1989, **"Bias in Human Reasoning. Causes and Consequences"**, Lawrence Erlbaum Associates, Hove UK.

Eysenck Michael, 1996, **"Simply Psychology"**, Psychology Press Publishers, Hove, East Sussex,

Fadiman James, Frager Robert, 1994, **"Personality, Personal Growth"**, Harpercollins College Publishers, New York.

Fineman Stephen (Ed), 1993, **"Emotion in Organisations"**, Sage Publications, London.

Fiske John, 1990, **"Introduction to Communication Studies"**, Routledge, London.

Forgas P Joseph (Ed), 1991, **"Emotion and Social Judgement"**, Pergamon press, Oxford.

Fuller Steve, 1988, **"Social Epistemology"**, Indiana University Press, United States of America.

Gellatly Angus (Ed), 1986, **"The Skilful Mind. An Introduction to Cognitive Psychology"**, Open University Press, Milton Keynes.

Gillette Jonathon, McCollon Manon (Ed), 1990, **"Groups in Context, A New Perspective on Group Dynamics"**, Addison-Wesley Publishing Company Inc, Canada.

Harre Rom, 1983, **"Personal Being"**, Basil Blackwell Publisher Limited, Oxford.

Hauert Claude-Alain (Ed), 1990, **"Developmental Psychology, Cognitive, Perceptuo-Motor and Neuropsychological Perspectives"**, Elsevier Science Publishers, New York.

Hayes Nicky, Orrell Sue, 1993, **"Psychology An Introduction"**, Longman Group UK Limited, London,

Jackendoff Ray, 1993, **"Patterns in the Mind, Language and Human Nature"**, Harvester Wheatsheaf, Hemel Hempstead, Hertfordshire.

Jung G Carl (Ed), 1964, **"Man and his Symbols"**, Aldus Books Ltd, London.

Klima Edward, Bellugi Ursula, 1979, **"The Signs of**

Language", Harvard University Press, United States of America.

Koehn Daryl, 1994, **"The Ground of Professional Ethics"**, Routledge, London,

Kyle JG, 1986, **"Sign Processes in Deaf People in Working Memory"**, School of Education Research Unit, University of Bristol, Bristol.

Kyle JG, Woll B, 1985, **"Sign Language, The study of deaf people and their language"**, Cambridge University Press, Northamptonshire.

Maglennon Keith, 1993, **"Essential Practical Psychology"**, Collins Educational Ltd, Hammersmith,

Marschark Marc, 1998, **"Mental Representation and Memory in Deaf Adults and Children"**, Rochester Institute of Technology, New York.

Martin Michael, Grover Brian, 1990, **"Ears and Hearing"**, Macdonald and Co Publishers Ltd, London,

Matlin W Margaret, 1983, **"Perception"**, Allyn and Bacon Inc, United States of America.

McIntire L Marina (Ed), 1986, **"Interpreting: The Art of Cross Cultural Mediation, Proceedings of the Ninth National Convention of the Registry of Interpreters for the Deaf July 4 - 8, 1985"**, RID Publications, Silver Spring, United States of America.

Mertens M Donna, 1998, **"Research Methods in Education and Psychology, Integrating Diversity with Quantitative and Qualitative Approaches"**, Sage Publications, London.

Miles Dorothy, 1988, **"British Sign Language. A Beginners Guide"**, BBC Books, London.

Moghaddam M Fathali, Taylor M Donald, Wright C Stephen, 1993, **"Social Psychology in Cross Cultural Perspective"**, W.H. Freeman and Company, United States of America.

Montgomery George (Ed), 1978, **"Deafness, Personality and Mental Health, Papers Presented to the Scottish Workshop with the Deaf"**, Scottish Workshop Publications, Edinburgh.

Ofshe J Richard (Ed), 1973, **"Interpersonal Behaviour in Small Groups"**, Prentice-Hall Inc, New Jersey.

Parasnis Ila (Ed) 1996, **"Cultural and Language Diversity and the Deaf Experience"**, Cambridge University Press, United States of America,

Peterson C Candida, Siegal Michael, 1995, **"Deafness, Conversation and Theory of Mind"** IN "J Child Psychology, Psychiatry", Vol. 36, No 3. pp. 459-474, 1995, Elsevier Science Ltd, Great Britain.

Rauch Irmengard, Carr F Gerald, 1980, **"The Signifying Animal"**, Indiana University press, United States of America,

Redfield James, Adrienne Carol, 1995, **"The Celestine Prophecy. An Experimental Guide"**, Bantam Books, Berkshire.

Roth Ilona (Ed), 1990, **"Introduction to Psychology, Second Edition"**, Lawrence Erlbaum Associates Ltd, Hove, East Surrey.

Sampson E Edward, 1991, **"Social Worlds, Personal Lives, An Introduction to Social Psychology"**, Harcourt Brace Jovanovich Publishers, Orlando.

Seleskovitch Danica, 1978, **"Interpreting for**

International conferences", Pen and Booth, Washington.

Shaw E Marvin, 1971, **"Group Dynamics, the Psychology of Small Group Behaviour"**, Mcgraw-Hill Inc, United States of America.

Smith B Peter, 1980, **"Group Processes"**, Harper and Row Ltd, London.

Spinelli Ernesto, 1995, **"The Interpreted World, An Introduction to Phenomenological Psychology"**, Sage Publications Inc, London.

Steiner B, 1997, **Lecture Notes,** Wolverhampton,

Stevens Anthony, 1994, **"Jung"**, Oxford University Press, Oxford.

Stewart A David, Schen D Jerome, Cartwright E Brenda, 1998, **"Sign Language Interpreting. Exploring its Art and Culture"**, Allyn and Bacon, Needham Heights.

Tervoort T Bernard (Ed), 1986, **"Signs of Life, Proceedings of the Second European Congress on sign Language Research"**, The Institute of General Linguistics of the University of Amsterdam, Amsterdam,

Wagner A Daniel, Stevenson W Harold, 1982, **"Cultural Perspectives on Child Development"**, W.H. Freeman and Company, United States of America.

Woll B (Ed), 1989, **"Language Development and Sign Language"**, International Sign Linguistics Association, Bristol.

Yule George, 1996, **"The Study of Language, Second Edition"**, Cambridge University Press, Cambridge.

Institute of Linguists Code of Professional Conduct, London, Transworld Linguist Services, London.

Printed in the United Kingdom
by Lightning Source UK Ltd.
9640300001BD/1